STEM Makerspace Projects

MAKERSPACE PROJECTS FOR
UNDERSTANDING ROBOTS

BROOKS BUTLER HAYS

PowerKiDS
press
New York

Published in 2021 by The Rosen Publishing Group, Inc.
29 East 21st Street, New York, NY 10010

First Edition

Editor: Danielle Haynes
Book Design: Reann Nye
Illustrator: Benjamin Humeniuk

Photo Credits: Series art (background) ShutterStockStudio/Shutterstock.com; cover, p. 9 asharkyu/Shutterstock.com; p. 5 LightField Studios/Shutterstock.com; p. 7 Suwin/Shutterstock.com; p. 11 Alexander Ryumin/TASS/Getty Images; p. 12 Ralph Crane/The LIFE Picture Collection/Getty Images; p. 13 JCDH/Shutterstock.com; p. 15 AndriyShevchuk/Shutterstock.com; p. 17 vrx/Shutterstock.com; p. 21 MONOPOLY919/Shutterstock.com; p. 25 Andrey Armyagov/Shutterstock.com; p. 29 Peter Cade/Stone/Getty Images.

Some of the images in this book illustrate individuals who are models. The depictions do not imply actual situations or events.

Library of Congress Cataloging-in-Publication Data

Names: Hays, Brooks Butler, author.
Title: Makerspace projects for understanding robots / Brooks Hays.
Description: New York : PowerKids Press, [2021] | Series: STEM makerspace
  projects | Includes bibliographical references and index.
Identifiers: LCCN 2019040328 | ISBN 9781725311862 (paperback) | ISBN
  9781725311886 (library binding) | ISBN 9781725311879 | ISBN
  9781725311893 (6 pack)
Subjects: LCSH: Robots–Juvenile literature. | Makerspaces–Juvenile
  literature.
Classification: LCC TJ211.2 .H425 2021 | DDC 629.8/92–dc23
LC record available at https://lccn.loc.gov/2019040328

Manufactured in the United States of America

CPSIA Compliance Information: Batch #CSPK20. For Further Information contact Rosen Publishing, New York, New York at 1-800-237-9932.

Find us on

CONTENTS

WHAT IS A MAKERSPACE?

A makerspace is someplace where people of all ages can gather to learn and work together to create projects. It's a place where learners can share ideas and bring a do-it-yourself spirit to education.

These spaces often have a variety of tools, **technologies**, and materials used to make, create, and inspire. The tools don't have to be complicated. You can use cardboard, tape, scissors, and glue—things found in most homes and classrooms—to craft your own adventures in learning.

To be human is to create, and to create is to learn and understand. Makerspaces are places where it's safe to take risks and try new things. They're places where young learners (and all learners) can meet and socialize.

Makerspaces are places where many different people can work together to make things, solve problems, and learn about creating.

INTRODUCTION TO ROBOTS

In movies and on television, robots often appear and behave like humans. In reality, however, robots come in all sorts of shapes, and most don't look particularly **humanoid**.

So, what are robots, exactly? Robots are machines that can perform a **complex** series of actions **automatically**. Using a computer, people can program some robots to move and work. Robots are autonomous, meaning they can operate independently and make some decisions for themselves.

There are robots that look, talk, move, and act a lot like humans. Every year, engineers build robots that are more and more humanlike. But there are far more robots that you might not think of as robots, including some kitchen appliances and automated vacuum cleaners.

Everyday Robots

You probably see and interact with robots regularly. If you've ever used an elevator to go up several flights of stairs, you've used a robot. If you've ever set your **thermostat** to control the temperature in your home, you've used a robot. In millions of homes across the country—perhaps even in yours—robotic vacuums keep floors free of dirt and dust. Robots come in all shapes and sizes, and they can be used to complete a variety of helpful tasks.

MAKER MAGIC

The word "robot" is derived from the Czech word *robota*, which translates as "forced labor" or "slave." Czech writer Karel Čapek was the first person to use the word "robot" in his 1920 play *R.U.R.: Rossum's Universal Robots*.

HISTORY OF AUTOMATA

Humans have been engineering robot-like machines, or automata, for centuries. The Egyptians developed a water clock as early as 1500 BC. The clock, once filled with water, emptied at a **predictable** pace, allowing watchers to tell the time. The force of the draining water caused small figures on the clock to strike bells each hour.

In 300 BC, Archytas, a Greek mathematician, built the world's first **self-propelled** flying device, a steam-powered wooden pigeon. About 1500, Leonardo da Vinci designed a mechanical knight operated by a series of simple machines. It could stand, sit, and open and close its helmet.

George Devol created the first industrial robot in 1954. It transported parts and attached them to automobile frames.

MAKER MAGIC

As of early 2018, South Korea led the world in robot density, which is the number of industrial robots per 10,000 workers. There are 631 industrial robots per 10,000 workers in the country, more than three times the number in the United States, which has the seventh-highest density.

The roots of robotics can be traced back centuries, but intelligent, autonomous robots have only been around for a few decades.

ROBOTS AT WORK

Today, many industries are becoming more automated. Over the past century, humans have **integrated** robots into thousands of factories. The machines have taken over repetitive and sometimes dangerous work previously done by humans.

Robotic arms assist humans on assembly lines all over the world. They help build TVs, cars, rockets, and more. Though some people fear their jobs will be taken by robots, automated machines could complete lower-skilled, low-paying tasks to free up human workers to take on more complicated, higher-paying duties.

Most industrial robots do highly specialized work and operate out of public view. However, robotics engineers are working to develop more skilled and interactive robots that can perform service work, such as cleaning hotel rooms or preparing food. In Japan, robots are already waiting tables at restaurants.

MAKER MAGIC

Robots might be coming to a classroom near you. At an early childhood education center in San Diego, California, school officials put a robot to work as a teaching assistant. It sings and helps teach children new words.

While some robots can help teachers in the classroom, others assist children unable to go to school.

ROBOT OR NOT?

Not everyone agrees on just what a robot is. Sometimes complex machines are said to be robots. However, while complex machines can accomplish tasks, they don't necessarily do so autonomously. Under another definition, a machine must show greater levels of **sophistication** and autonomy to be a robot.

MAKER MAGIC

The first modern robot to be intelligent, autonomous, and capable of making its own decisions was named Shakey. Engineers at Stanford University designed and unveiled the robot in 1966.

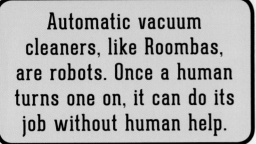

Automatic vacuum cleaners, like Roombas, are robots. Once a human turns one on, it can do its job without human help.

Many robotic engineers consider a robot to be somewhere in between. One popular way to determine whether a complex machine is a robot is to think about whether it can sense, compute, and act. If it can, then it's a robot.

Robots can differ in shape, size, and level of sophistication and specialization. However, they all use **sensors** that send messages to a computer, which processes those messages and sends signals to a motor that powers the moving parts.

13

DIY BOTS

Building a robot requires hardware and software that many makerspaces don't have. However, you can still build robot-like devices, or bots—machines that look and move like a robot but don't necessarily think like a robot. In the chapters ahead, you'll learn how to create bots that are missing the kinds of intelligence or sensors that make a machine a robot but still give a window into the world of robotics.

Remember, for a machine to be a robot, it must be able to sense its surroundings, make decisions based on those senses, and take action. Even though they don't act entirely like robots, the bots you'll learn to build in the chapters ahead could be outfitted with the software and sensors needed to turn them into robots.

Anyone can learn the basic building blocks of robotics.

SWARMING BOTS

Swarming robots are inspired by insects, such as bees and ants, that live in colonies. Individually, bees and ants aren't all that bright, but together, the colonies can show an impressive intelligence. Swarming robots behave similarly, using shared intelligence to sense their surroundings and accomplish basic tasks.

Engineers are working with medical researchers to create swarms of tiny robots, or nanobots, to deliver helpful drugs and attack harmful cells inside the human body.

In the next chapter, you'll learn how to build a bot called a brush bot. A vibrating motor powers the bot. Its brush can be used to clean a surface. If you build a dozen brush bots and supply them with sensory abilities and collective intelligence, you'd have a robotic swarm of cleaning bots.

Nature and Robots

Robotics engineers take many of their ideas from nature. By studying the movement and behavior patterns of swarming or flocking animals such as birds and bees, scientists can learn how to program swarming robots to **coordinate** their movements. When engineers need to develop a robot that swims or jumps, for example, they often study the mechanics of animals that can swim very fast or jump really high.

Nanobots are so small that they can travel inside the human body to affect cells.

PROJECT 1:
MAKE A BRUSH BOT

You can use your brush bot to scrub a surface clean or to race another brush bot.

WHAT YOU NEED

- two AA batteries
- double AA battery holder
- 3-volt DC motor

- scrub brush
- double-sided foam tape
- electrical tape

- cork
- small Phillips-head screwdriver
- scissors

WHAT YOU WILL DO

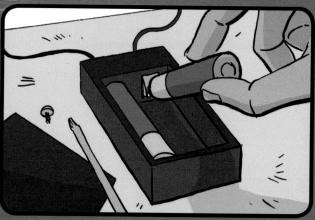

STEP 1:
Remove the door on the battery holder. You may need to use the screwdriver to remove the door. Put the batteries in the battery holder and reattach the door.

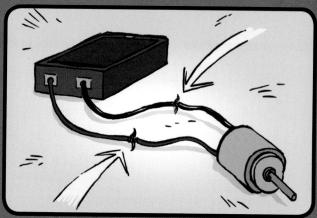

STEP 2:
Attach the wires from the battery holder to the 3-volt DC motor by twisting the wires together. Match the red wires together and the black wires together. Wrap some electrical tape around each wire where they're connected.

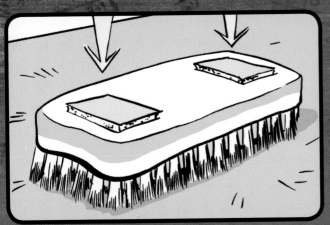

STEP 3:

Apply two pieces of double-sided foam tape to the top of the scrub brush.

STEP 4:

Secure the battery holder to one of the pieces of foam tape.

STEP 5:

Secure the motor to the other piece of tape. Make sure the motor's rotor, or the part that rotates, is facing the back of the brush and extends out over the edge.

STEP 6:

Stick the cork onto the motor's rotor so that it can spin freely without bumping the edge of the brush.

STEP 7:

To make sure the motor doesn't fly off when you turn it on, you can add a strip of electrical tape over the top to secure it to the brush.

STEP 8:

Switch the motor on and watch the scrub brush vibrate across the table.

ROBOTS AND MOTION

Robots have bodies that can move or take physical actions. This is unlike so-called "web robots," which live on the Internet and scan and collect data and perform virtual actions online.

To take action, robots need **components** called actuators. Actuators trigger movement. They can be powered by electricity, or air (pneumatic) or water (hydraulic) pressure. Actuators are to robots what muscles are to people. Robots capable of complex movements rely on multiple actuators.

Actuators convert energy and signals into motion, causing a device or robot to perform an action.

In the next chapter, you'll learn to build a simple motor, a type of actuator, which can turn electricity into movement—the kind of movement a robot could use to accomplish a task.

MAKER MAGIC

Engineers at the robotics company Boston Dynamics built a robot named Atlas that can do a backflip. Not to be one-upped, engineers at Massachusetts Institute of Technology programmed their four-legged robot, named Mini Cheetah, to do one too.

For a machine to be a robot, it must have a body that's capable of performing physical action. It has to move.

SCANNING IN PROGRESS

PROJECT 2: MAKE A SIMPLE MOTOR

Robots must perform physical actions. Motors power movement. If you can build a simple motor, you can build all kinds of motorized devices, including robots.

WHAT YOU NEED

- coated copper wire
- AA battery
- two paper clips, metal and uninsulated
- magnet
- small block of wood, about 3 inches by 3 inches across the top
- pliers
- scissors
- sandpaper
- glue
- small nail
- hammer

WHAT YOU WILL DO

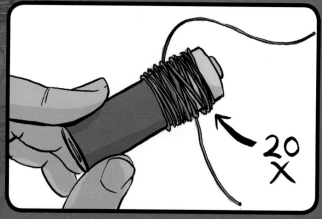

STEP 1:

Start by making a coil of copper wire. Wrap the coil at least 20 times around the battery, making sure to leave a couple inches of extra wire on each end of the coil. Slide the coil off the battery.

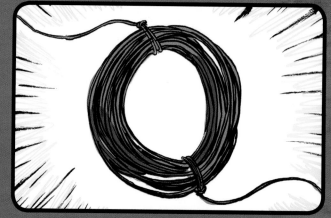

STEP 2:

To keep the wire from uncoiling, use the ends of spare wire to tie two knots around the coil. Make sure there is still some wire left over after tying the knots.

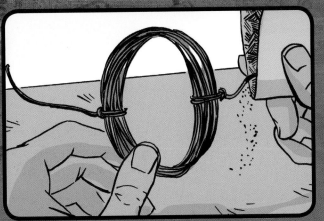

STEP 3:

Use sandpaper to remove the coating entirely from one end of the spare wire that's sticking out from the coil. Use sandpaper to remove the bottom half of the insulation from the other spare end of wire. (Leave insulation on the top.)

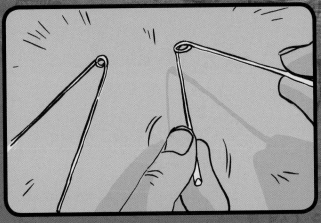

STEP 4:

Use the pliers to straighten and bend the paper clips so that each forms a "V" shape with a small loop at the bend.

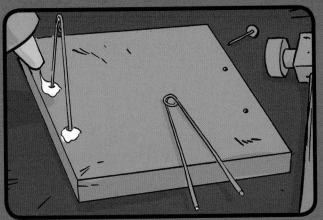

STEP 5:

Use the hammer and nail to make four small, shallow holes—two on each end of the top, flat side of the piece of wood. Each pair of holes should be about a half-inch apart and line up with the pair on the other side of the wood. The pairs of holes should be about 2 inches apart. Secure the ends of the paper clips in each pair of holes using glue.

STEP 6:

Thread the two ends of the coiled wire through the loops at the top of each paper clip. The coil should be suspend between the two paper clips.

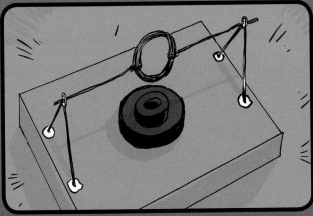

STEP 7:

Put one or two magnets on the wood block so that they are positioned just beneath the copper loop.

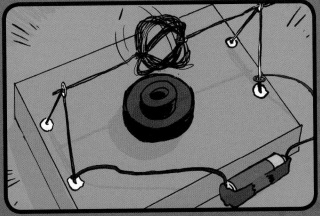

STEP 8:

Attach the ends of two separate copper wires to the base of each paper clip. Hold the other ends of those wires to the battery, one at each end of the battery. Watch the block vibrate as the coil spins.

AIR AND ROBOTS

As we've discussed, robots must be able to take action. They need to move. There are different ways to power robotic motion. One way involves air. When a compressed gas (such as air) is used to power an actuator, it's called pneumatic motion.

When a gas is compressed, or pressurized, it stores energy. When the compressed air is released, it creates a force. When you blow up a balloon, you're compressing air inside the balloon. When you release the balloon's air, you're producing a pneumatic force.

A pneumatic system requires several things: an air compressor to create air; a reservoir, or place to store air; **valves** to control air; a circuit through which air can move into other components; and a motor that can be powered by the air.

MAKER MAGIC

Pneumatic motion is especially important for soft robots. The use of compressed air to power motion allows soft robots to move more smoothly—to slither like a snake or scoot like a worm.

Compressed air and pneumatic systems power the movements of many kinds of robots and complex machines.

PROJECT 3:
BUILD A ROBOTIC GRIPPER

You don't need a hand with fingers to grip and hold different objects, just a balloon, some coffee, and a vacuum.

WHAT YOU NEED

- small electric reversible vacuum pump (used for air mattresses)
- balloon
- coarsely ground coffee
- kitchen funnel, about 3 inches in diameter
- duct tape
- small piece of breathable fabric
- small objects to pick up using robotic gripper

WHAT YOU WILL DO

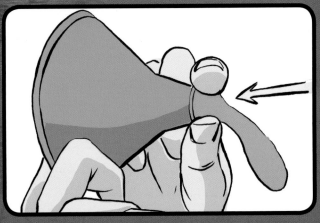

STEP 1:
Slip the opening of the balloon over the narrow end of the funnel.

STEP 2:
Fill the balloon with coffee grounds by pouring the coffee into the wide end of the funnel. There should be enough grounds in the balloon that when you place the filled balloon inside the big opening of the funnel, it sticks out of the funnel slightly. (See next step.)

STEP 3:

When the balloon is full, take the balloon off the small end of the funnel. Put the balloon in the bigger end of the funnel, threading the opening of the balloon through the narrow end of the funnel. To secure the balloon to the funnel, invert the opening of the balloon around the small opening of the funnel.

STEP 4:

To keep the coffee grounds inside the balloon, place a small piece of breathable fabric over the balloon's opening. Use duct tape to secure the fabric to the balloon and the balloon to the funnel. The fabric acts as a filter to let air pass through but keep the grounds in place.

STEP 5:

Attach the vacuum pump hose to the small end of the funnel using the duct tape. Use a lot of tape to make sure the seal is airtight.

STEP 6:

To pick up an object, partially inflate the balloon with the vacuum pump. While the balloon is inflated and the coffee grounds are loose inside, press the balloon against an object you want to pick up.

STEP 7:

Now reverse the vacuum so it sucks the extra air out of the balloon, causing the grounds to tighten around object you want to pick up. Now lift the end of the vacuum pump/balloon and you'll see the object attached to the balloon!

STEP 8:

To release the object from the grip of the balloon, turn off the vacuum.

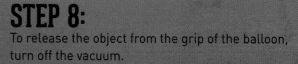

IMAGINING ROBOTS

Now that you understand the building blocks of robots, you can begin to think about the ways new kinds of robots could help solve everyday problems. When you're going about your day, think about ways you can use robots to make life easier. Identify a problem, such as a chore you hate to do, and think about how you would design a robot to do that work. Think about how you might be able to combine the kinds of projects you just built into a robot capable of helping you out.

When outside, look at the animals you see—the birds in the trees or the frogs in a pond. Think about the ways those animals move and how that can be used in construction of a new robot.

MAKER MAGIC

Leonardo da Vinci was a great inventor, and he built several robotic-like devices. But he never built a real robot. You don't have to build a robot to engage with robotics. You can think about and draw robots, just like Leonardo.

All robots start out as ideas. They're figments of an inventor's imagination and sketches on a notepad long before they're actually built.

COMPUTERS, CODING, AND ROBOTS

If you're interested in robotics, enjoy making things, and would like to make a real robot in the future, you're going to need to learn a bit about computers and programming. Robots that are autonomous still rely on software that's programmed by humans.

To be a robotics engineer, you'll need to learn some computer coding. There are hundreds of computer programming languages you can learn.

Makerspaces offer a place to work and create with your friends and classmates, but not all makerspaces have the types of technologies or learning resources needed to program software and integrate it with a robot. Ask your teachers and parents to help you find places and people that can teach you about coding robotic software.

GLOSSARY

automatically: Having controls that allow something to act without being directed by a person.

complex: Having many parts.

component: A part of a larger whole.

coordinate: To work together well.

humanoid: Resembling a human.

integrate: Combine one thing with another to form a whole.

predictable: Behaving in a way that is expected.

self-propelled: Able to be moved without external help.

sensor: A device that detects something and sends information to something else.

sophistication: Having a high degree of complexity.

technology: A method that uses science to solve problems and the tools used to solve those problems.

thermostat: A device that helps control temperature.

valve: A device that opens and closes to control the flow of a liquid or gas.

INDEX

WEBSITES

Due to the changing nature of Internet links, PowerKids Press has developed an online list of websites related to the subject of this book. This site is updated regularly. Please use this link to access the list: www.powerkidslinks.com/stemmake/robots